Profit Strategies:
Unlocking Trading Performance With Money Management

David Stendahl

TRADE SECRETS

Profit Strategies:
Unlocking Trading
Performance with
Money Management

DAVID STENDAHL

ISBN 1-883272-30-0

Printed in the United States of America.

CONTENTS

SPECIAL THANKS

I would like to especially thank James Goldcamp, Leo Zamansky and Terry Carr for their help and guidance developing many of the concepts and tools used throughout this book.

In addition, special mention is deserved for the many authors, experts and colleagues who have influenced this work including: Tim Slater, Walter Bressert, Ralph Vince, Jack Schwager, John Sweeney, Robert Deel, Mark Jurik, Curtis Stendahl, Sunny Harris, Averill Strasser, John Boyer and the numerous individuals at Omega Research.

TRADING DISCLAIMER

Trading involves risk including possible loss of principal and other losses. Your trading results may vary. Trading futures involves risk and may not be suited for all traders. No representation is being made that any account will or is likely to achieve profits similar to those shown. RINA Systems' products and services are intended for use as a tool by traders to assist and enhance various approaches to trading.

Preface

Traders can typically describe the methods they use to initiate and liquidate trades. However, when forced to describe a methodology for the amount of capital to risk when trading few traders have a concrete answer. Some make vague references to expert's that recommend risking one or two percent of portfolio equity on any trade. Others rely on intuition to determine when to increase position size on a particular trade, always risking different amounts. Experienced traders learn, however, that as important as it is to have an effective method to determine when to trade, it is equally important to develop a methodology to determine how much to risk. A trader that risks too much increases the chance that he will not survive long enough to realize the long run benefits of a valid trading strategy. However, risking too little creates the possibility that a trading methodology may not realize its full potential. Therefore, while a positive expectation may be a minimal requirement to trade successfully, the way in which you are able to exploit that positive expectation will in large part determine your success as a trader. This is, in fact, one of the greatest challenges for traders.

At RINA Systems, we have had the fortune of working with many experienced traders, and in that process we became increasingly aware of the need for sound methods for applying money management strategies. In fact, it seems that as traders reach a certain level of comfort with a system they begin to realize that a sound money management approach is missing from their trading strategy. Our work in this area has led us to research several strategies for determining position size and ways in which to add to, decrease, and stop out positions. Many of these strategies are well known and readily available in the public domain and others are hybrids that we have built from improving concepts already available. Moreover, once you understand the importance of money management, the opportunity to modify many of the well-known strategies to meet your needs is endless.

It is our belief that there is really no "black box" formula for money management. That is, different trading strategies and systems require different approaches to money management. In addition, we must always consider the trader's ability to implement a money management strategy given his tolerance for risk and other psychological factors. For example, several strategies that emphasize optimizing the amount of capital to invest in a trade to achieve maximum returns often deliver substantial drawdowns. Few traders are comfortable suffering through a draw-down of fifty, sixty, or seventy percent, which is not unheard of for some aggressive strategies. Therefore, it is essential to match the theoretical drawdown with the trader's ability to tolerate it.

Finally, and not insignificant, is that a trader's capitalization may affect his ability to execute a strategy. Even in cases where it might be preferable from a system performance perspective to utilize a money management strategy that tends to add to positions as the price moves against the trader, an undercapitalized trader may be unable to add to positions during a drawdown in equity while in a trade. In this situation the trader would be unable to derive the potential benefits of the strategy.

Therefore, apart from the effectiveness of a particular strategy on a given trading methodology, there are two important variables: the psychological preferences of the trader and his level of capitalization. If either of these two factors does not support the money management strategy employed, then it is unlikely the trader will be able to use the strategy effectively. Though seemingly insignificant, this point cannot be overemphasized, because many strategies are developed over large histories of data (in many cases 10 or 20 years of data). The trader needs to have the confidence to remain with the strategy even if positive results do not come immediately.

We believe that you will benefit from the strategies presented in this guide. In addition, we hope we have created a greater awareness for the need to evaluate what type of money management system you are using. Hopefully, we will spur your imagination when thinking about ways in which to use money management.

We find that many traders focus much of their creativity on entry and exit logic. However, a range of methods for determining position size can be employed and traders are well advised to devote considerable effort in determining this as well.

It should be noted that all traders are using some form of money management. Some, though, are not conscious of what type of strategy or method they are using. Other traders use thought out and tested methodologies for determining how much capital to commit to trades and sound strategies for adding to or exiting positions, which are consistent with their expectations of risk. It is our hope that you will find yourself among the latter group.

Introduction

The goal of this book is to explain the process by which traders can develop, evaluate and ultimately improve the performance of trading systems with money management strategies. These improvements must be based on an individual's risk tolerance and trading psychology. At RINA Systems we have developed an evaluation and improvement process to address these issues.

We believe that money management does not exist in a vacuum. This means that it is essential that your money management strategy be integrated into an overall approach to system design and development. Therefore, before we move directly into the application of various money management strategies we will focus on some elementary issues concerning system design and testing. We believe this is an essential component in our approach to money management. To provide you with an adequate foundation to apply money management we will take you through the necessary stages of development that precede the application of money management. It is a requirement that the trader sufficiently understands the methodology being employed and where it's likely to succeed or fail.

To assist in our evaluation we will present an analysis that has been derived using MoneyManager and 3D SmartView from RINA Systems and Portfolio Maximizer, a product co-developed by RINA Systems and Omega Research.

While many approaches and strategies to money management are available, in this book we will focus on the money and risk management strategies listed below:

- Maximum Adverse Excursion

- Maximum Favorable Excursion

- Drawdown Support

- Winning Series

- Fixed Fractional

- Optimal f

- Secure f

In addition, we will combine some of these strategies to create a fully integrated approach to money and risk management. Once again, we do not claim nor intend to cover all of the strategies for money and risk management available to traders. We do, however, strive to present a useful overview of several techniques available to traders to achieve effective money management methodology.

Before we get into the details, let's take this opportunity to briefly discuss the chapters we will cover in this book.

In chapter one, we will design a methodology to trade the currency markets using continuous price data. In addition, we will center on developing and programming the system using TradeStation by Omega Research. It should be noted, however, that many of our examples could also be implemented in Microsoft Excel or other spreadsheet applications.

In chapter two, we will begin evaluating the stability of our trading system. We will use three-dimensional graphs to help evaluate the robustness of our Deutsche Mark trading system. Once again, this type of analysis can be accomplished using a variety of spreadsheet or advanced mathematics packages available.

In chapter three, we will evaluate the system's performance to determine if the trading characteristics of the system fit our psychological profile. We will use Portfolio Maximizer, an evaluation package co-developed by RINA Systems and Omega Research, to assist in our detailed system evaluation. This detailed evaluation will be invaluable as we begin applying our money management strategies.

The process of improving the performance of the system by applying money, risk, and equity management strategies is addressed in the fourth chapter. We will build on the evaluation stage by testing a number of money and risk management techniques to determine which strategies work best with our system.

This stage is critical to making significant improvements to the performance of our Deutsche Mark system.

In chapter five, we will conclude our discussion of money management by analyzing the performance of our portfolio to ensure that a risk-adjusted portfolio is created. Issues relating to diversification and the way systems interact in a portfolio are discussed.

In summary, we will design a simple trading system, evaluate its performance, and ultimately improve its results using a variety of money management strategies.

Although the focus of this book is on money management, it is important to realize that it is imperative to know as much about our system as possible to justify applying specific money management strategies. This implies that we fully evaluate our system's design and performance prior to applying any form of money management. Once the evaluation is complete we can apply appropriate money management strategies with a high degree of confidence that our system's performance results will be improved in accordance with our risk tolerance.

Profit Strategies:

Unlocking Trading Performance With Money Management

chapter 1
System Design

The goal of *Profit Strategies*, is to introduce and apply a systematic process of developing, evaluating, and improving trading systems. Once you understand this process you can apply it to any number of systems or trading ideas you may have.

The sample system we have selected is a simple moving average crossover system that trades the Deutsche Mark. If we are able to design a profitable system using this methodology then imagine what you can do with more complex trading systems and methodologies. By using a simple system in particular, we do not have to spend a lot of time on the system itself, but rather we can spend our time on the process of evaluation and improvement, which is, after all, the goal of this book.

Our base system, once taken through the evaluation and money management process, will generate superior performance, especially on such a simple system. The actual improvement will increase the system's net profit by over 635%. This is a huge increase given the fact that we are designing a simple moving average trading system. The net result will be a stable system that is highly profitable and easy to trade.

The first step in designing a system is to evaluate what type of market we are trading. Markets basically come in two types: Trending and Non-trending. Each of these markets will have it's own personality.

TRENDING VS. NON-TRENDING MARKETS

Trending markets have a tendency to move in the same direction for extended periods of time in either a bullish or bearish

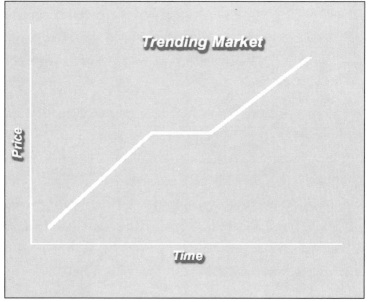

Exhibit 1: Trending Market

manner. The currencies are an example of markets that often exhibit this trending behavior. To illustrate this, let's look at a graphic of a trending market.

Notice that once the market begins its trend it typically moves in the same direction for a long period of time. Trending markets are typically traded with breakout or moving average systems. This type of system never catches the exact top or bottom of a market, but rather aims to remain with the general trend. Trending systems do not necessarily generate a lot of winning trades, but when they experience a profitable trade it is typically quite large.

Non-trending markets, like the financials, have a tendency to make quick moves reversing direction at the drop of a dime. Our next exhibit illustrates a non-trending market.

Notice how the market appears to be locked between support and resistance levels. These levels help determine when the market is overbought or oversold. Non-trending markets are typically traded with momentum indicators such as RSI, %R, and CCI as well as a host of other rate-of-change based indicators. These systems attempt to catch the tops and bottoms and typically have a higher percentage of winning trades than trending systems. Non-trending systems are capable of generating a large number of consistently profitable trades.

Evaluation Tip

RINA Systems' Dynamic Zone indicator works exceptionally well with non-trending markets. For more information on the Dynamic Zone indicator refer to our article "Dynamic Zone " published in the July 97 issue of *Technical Analysis of Stocks and Commodities.*

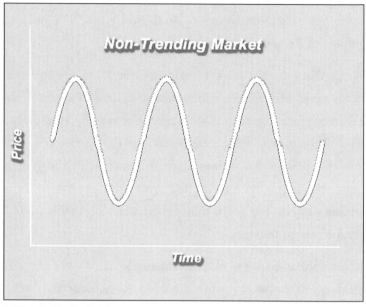

Exhibit 2: Non-Trending Market

By reviewing the underlying market we can determine whether it's trending or non-trending. Now bear in mind that all markets, whether they are futures, stocks, or mutual funds, exhibit signs of being both trending and non-trending. What we are talking about here is the market's primary nature -- is it typically trending or non-trending? Once we know what we are dealing with, developing our primary system is a lot easier and a great deal more profitable.

We are attempting to ensure that our methodology is consistent with the behavior of the underlying market. Attempting to use a long-term trend-following system on a choppy market generally does not work. It is for this reason that every system may not be appropriate for every market.

Since we will be trading the Deutsche Mark, we will want to design a system that is primarily trend-following oriented. The system will be based on a simple moving average crossover that will attempt to capture the majority of the larger trends in the Deutsche Mark.

Now that we know a little more about the trading characteristics of our market we are ready to develop the trading system.

CROSSOVER METHODOLOGY

We begin with the typical crossover system that goes long the market when the faster moving average crosses the slower moving average. The system remains long until the moving average crosses in the opposite direction causing the system to short the market.

Let's take a look at a graphic to better understand our trading logic.

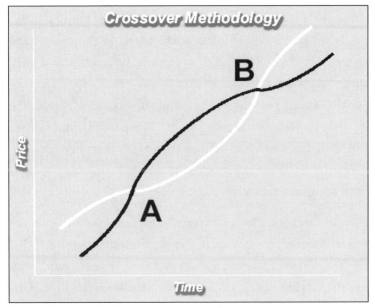

Exhibit 3: Crossover Methodology

The system goes long at point A where the moving averages cross in a positive manner. And at point B the system reverses and goes short as the moving averages cross again in a negative manner. The system initiates a new trade every time the moving averages cross one another.

This basically describes our trading methodology but already there is a conceptual flaw that will affect the long-term performance of our system. This flaw centers on how the system trades the long and short side of the market.

GREED AND FEAR DESCRIPTION

Let's explain the need to develop a methodology for both the long and short side in a little more detail. No matter which market you trade, all markets are affected by human nature: greed and fear. Markets have a tendency to move in a direction for an extended period of time and then quickly reverse. The greedy nature of traders accounts for market trending in a certain direction whether it's bullish or bearish. Fear on the other hand accounts for the quick reversal of fortune. When the herd mentality of the market decides to change direction it may do so very quickly. Greed and fear help to explain why markets react the way they do to bull and bear moves. These bullish and bearish tendencies can be seen in all time frames whether they are short or long term. What is important to realize is that trading boils down to human nature: greed and fear.

If the markets are affected by greed and fear then so too is the system. The conceptual flaw in our system relates to the fact that our system trades long then short and then repeats again. Any time the moving averages cross one another we reverse our position. A reversal system that trades 100% of the time doesn't give us any opportunity to make adjustments at the system development stage. And for that matter, it will really affect us at the money management stage.

Because we want to design an effective trading system, - we will have to account for greed and fear in the development of our system. To do this we will develop two systems to trade the same market. One only goes long and the other short. Splitting the methodology into two systems allows us to evaluate and improve the individual systems and then combine them back together at the portfolio level. Developing systems separately for both the long and the short side gives us greater flexibility in evaluating and improving our system.

SYSTEM DEVELOPMENT PROCESS

We now have one more refinement to properly develop the trading system. This involves separating the entry and exit signals. There is no reason to believe that whatever logic got us into our trade is appropriate to exit the trade. Let's take a look at Exhibit 4 to see exactly how we are developing our system.

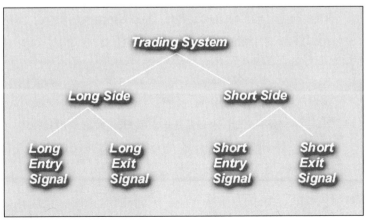

Exhibit 4: System Development Process

Whenever possible, we want to bring our system down to the lowest level, which in this case is the signal level. We have entry signals and exit signals for both our long system and short system. The entry and exit signals combine to create our separate long and short systems. These two separate systems are then combined to create our mini-portfolio. The net result is - we end up with a system that trades long and short but allows us to refine the system based on our robustness analysis, system evaluation and money management strategies.

TRADING SYSTEM CODE

Let's take a look at the code to our system to better understand how it trades. For the sake of time we will focus primarily on the Long side.

Exhibit 5: Long Moving Average Crossover System

```
Input: Length1(8), Length2(20), Length3(5), Length4(23);

IF CurrentBar > 1 and Average (Close, Length1) crosses over
Average (Close,Length2) Then Buy on Close;

IF CurrentBar > 1 and Average (Close, Length3) crosses below
Average (Close, Length4) Then ExitLong on Close;
```

Evaluation Tip

You can also use TradeStation's Moving Average system as a starting point for developing your own crossover system. The system can be found in the Power Editor under the name MovAvg Crossover.

We see that our system enters into a Long position when the Moving Average #1 crosses over Moving Average #2. The position is exited when Moving Average #3 crosses below Moving Average #4.

This system is very similar to every moving average system ever developed. We simply go a step further by breaking the system down to a lower level. Therefore, we have four inputs per system. As you can see at the top of Exhibit 5 the system inputs are Length 1 through Length 4, which correspond to the four moving averages. The short trading system shown below follows the same logic using separate moving averages to enter and exit its short positions.

Exhibit 6: Short Moving Average Crossover System

Input: Length1(5), Length2(20), Length3(12), Length4(15);

IF CurrentBar > 1 and Average (Close, Length1) crosses below Average (Close, Length2) Then Sell on Close;

IF CurrentBar > 1 and Average (Close, Length3) crosses over Average (Close, Length4) Then ExitShort on Close;

CHAPTER ONE SUMMARY

In summary, we have separated the long and short positions and refined the system by separating the entry and exit signals. These refinements will allow us to better evaluate the performance of the system. As you will see this is a key part to developing a profitable well-designed system.

chapter 2
Robustness Analysis

In this chapter we will conduct a detailed evaluation of our system. We will focus on evaluating the robustness of our system using three-dimensional graphs.

ROBUSTNESS ANALYSIS

Robustness analysis allows us to take the inputs for a system and evaluate them to determine the most stable settings. To accomplish this task we must optimize the system inputs in TradeStation. Our goal is not to optimize our trading system to generate the largest historical net profit, but rather use the optimization report to determine the stability of our system. An unstable trading system may appear to be historically sound, but eventually the system will fail due to subtle changes in the market over time. Therefore the more stable the system over a range of inputs, the more likely it is to maintain its performance in the future.

To help us assess our system's stability we will look at a variety of three-dimensional performance graphs. A few of the more important performance characteristics to consider are net profit, profit factor, the ratio of average wins to average loss, and drawdown. With robustness analysis we are able to understand our system's stability across all of these performance measures.

If we find that the system's net profit, for example, drops off dramatically by making a small change to the input value, then we know that the system is not very stable and may be susceptible to failure in the future. If, however, the system's performance is NOT highly sensitive to the system's settings, that is, small changes in inputs do not result in a large change in the net profit then we may feel more comfortable with the stability of the system. The point is that it's preferable to have a system perform well over a large range of values.

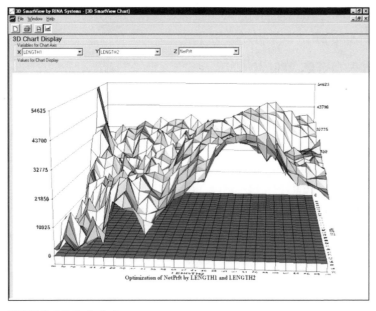

Exhibit 7: Unstable Trading System

Let's review the results of a trading system to better understand how to determine the robustness of a system. The system we are about to evaluate is not our moving average system but rather another system that allows us to easily see the difference between stable and non-stable trading results. Once we know what a bad system looks like it is easier to appreciate our stable Deutsche Mark system.

The results in Exhibit 7 reflect the net profit output for a trading system plotted on a three-dimensional graph. The system has been optimized generating a Net Profit figure for each of the system's inputs. Notice the rounded Net Profit section on the right hand side of the graphic. Any small adjustment made to the system's inputs has little effect on the net profit. The system's net profit ranges between $41,000 and $43,000. This amounts to less than a 5% deviation.

The left-hand side of the 3D SmartView graphic tells a different story. The system's net profit figure drops off dramatically with little adjustment made to the system's inputs. The system's optimized net profit figure generates a $54,000 net profit. But a slight adjustment to the inputs produces a net profit figure of $34,000 in one direction and $22,000 in another. That's a 40% and 63% decline in profitability, respectively, based on a small adjustment to the systems inputs.

We would hate to be trading this system with parameters set at the spike. The likelihood that the system will continue to trade at this level is very low. Selecting the inputs on the right hand side of Exhibit 7 will produce less of a historic net profit, but a much more stable system for trading in the future.

The bottom line is, the system is stable with certain input settings and very unstable with other settings. Evaluating your system using three-dimensional area graphs of a system's performance over a range of parameters is a tremendous aid in evaluating the robustness of your trading system.

OPTIMIZATION PROS AND CONS

Optimization can be your best friend or worst enemy. It all depends upon how you use it. Because it is often used incorrectly, optimization has a bad reputation. However, instead of using it to make the system look better from a historic perspective, we should use it to evaluate a system's sensitivity to changes in the underlying market.

It's always surprising when traders say that they don't use optimization because they don't want to fit their system to past data. Without analyzing the robustness of a system how do they know they haven't inadvertently selected highly unstable system parameter settings? Traders may make a conscious effort not to "fit" the data but through lack of testing actually DO fit their system to the past. Performing a simple robustness analysis on a system will go a long way to ensuring that curve fitting is minimized.

CLUSTER ANALYSIS

We want to recognize, of course, that Net Profit is an important performance measure. However, we should also pay attention to several other measures of performance. Robustness analysis involves reviewing the results of a number of performance related statistics including profit factor, percent profitable trades, the ratio of average wins to average losses, maximum draw-down, and several others. The goal is to find an area that offers stable trading results simultaneously across several system performance measures and several inputs. We call this process cluster analysis.

Let's return our attention to our Deutsche Mark system and implement what we have just learned.

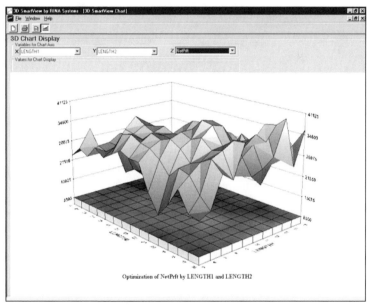

Exhibit 8: Stable Trading System based on Net Profit

Notice that our Deutsche Mark system generates stable results in the center of the graphic. If we were to evaluate the same system using all of our other performance measures they would all point to the same area. Take a look at our average trade 3D Graphic to refine our robustness analysis.

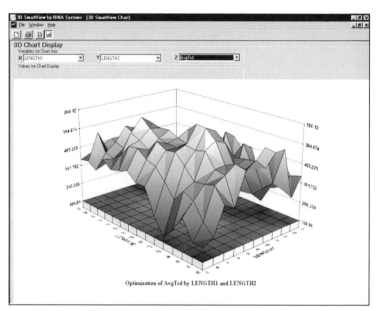

Exhibit 9: Stable Trading System based on Average Trade

Evaluation Tip
These inputs were used to generate the trading results for both our long and short Deutsche Mark trading system.

Based on our robustness analysis we have selected the following inputs for our Deutsche Mark trading system.

Long Moving Average Crossover System Inputs

Input: Length1(8),Length2(20), Length3(5),Length4(23);

Short Moving Average Crossover System Inputs

Input: Length1(5),Length2(20), Length3(12),Length4(15);

CHAPTER TWO SUMMARY

Having used three-dimensional graphs to determine robust trading inputs we can now move on to the next chapter and evaluate the performance of our system with a higher degree of confidence.

chapter 3
System Evaluation

Performing a system evaluation is critical to the design and development of a trading system. Traders need to assess their system's true performance in order to build confidence in the system.

The rationale for a detailed evaluation is simple -- every trader has his or her own idea as to what makes a great trading system. A system that is preferable to one person may not be appropriate for another. It's not uncommon to hear two traders talk about the same trading system that one loves and the other hates. This difference of opinion is most likely attributed to their individual trading styles. For example, one trader may be aggressive while the other is conservative. Because a system is historically profitable doesn't necessarily mean that the system is suited to that trader.

At RINA Systems we talk to a lot of traders that say, "I know my system is good because it makes money." That factor alone may not be indicative of a system that is compatible with your trading style. The reality is a conservative trader will likely not be able to tolerate the volatility that is inherent with many aggressive strategies. As well, an aggressive trader may not have the patience to remain with a conservative system. Both systems may be profitable, but just not suited to that particular trader. Understanding how you relate to your trading system is perhaps the most important element in trading.

One factor you will want to keep in mind is that we have the ability to adjust how aggressive or conservative a system is through the use of money management. Therefore, it is not always necessary to think about whether the system is aggressive or conservative in the development stage. What we do need, however, is a well-designed and stable trading system to be able to subsequently improve it with money management.

It is for this reason we perform a thorough and complete evaluation to assess the strengths and weakness of a system BEFORE we trade it. The better prepared an individual is to trade, the better chance they have of becoming a successful trader. In the end it is up to the individual to decide if the system is worth trading. No matter how profitable a system appears, if he doesn't have the ability to stick with the system during periods of poor performance or sufficient capital to survive drawdowns, then he should look for another system to trade. There are plenty to choose from - the goal is, find the one that is most correct for the individual.

The remainder of this chapter will concentrate on the evaluation tools offered in Portfolio Maximizer. The performance statistics presented in Portfolio Maximizer are divided into a number of sections. Each section dissects the system's performance from a different perspective.

EVALUATION PROCESS

The evaluation process begins with a general overview of the system's performance. We then begin to focus on specific areas of performance, from which we can make improvements. The entire evaluation process is comprised of the following sections:

> **Evaluation Tip**
> RINA Systems created a two tape video series with Omega Research entitled "A Guide to Testing and Evaluating Portfolios with Portfolio Maximizer" to cover the evaluation process in greater detail.

- System Analysis

- Total Trades

- Profit Ratios

- Outlier Trades

- Return Figures

- Drawdown/Run-up

- Trading Summary

- Consecutive Trades

- Equity Curve Analysis

- Time Analysis

Each of these sections will help us fully evaluate and ultimately improve our Deutsche Mark trading system.

MAXIMUM ADVERSE EXCURSION

Evaluation Tip

Maximum Adverse Excursion is a money management strategy that limits our system's exposure to large drawdowns.

Before we begin evaluating our Deutsche Mark system we must apply some form of stop logic to ensure the safety of our trading capital. The process we will use to find and set appropriate stop levels is called Maximum Adverse Excursion or MAE for short. This process was introduced to traders by John Sweeney of *Technical Analysis of Stocks and Commodities* magazine, and is a great tool for finding appropriate levels to place stops.

MAE allows us to evaluate our system's individual trades to determine at what dollar or percentage amount to place our protective stop. Let's take a look at how to use the MAE graphic to properly place our stop.

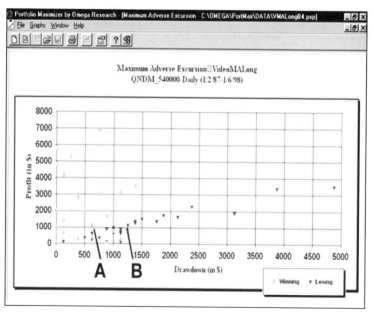

Exhibit 10: Maximum Adverse Excursion

This graphic shows all 59 trades that make up our Deutsche Mark system. For each trade we can see the amount of draw-down that occurred in relation to realized prof-it or loss. The winning trades are shown as light up arrows and the losing trades are repre-sented as dark down arrows. Since we are using this graphic to determine where to place our stops we have put all the winning and los-ing trades on the same cluster graph. This means that although Trades A and B appear to be similar they are in reality quite different. Trade A had a drawdown of $600 before recovering to net a profit of $1,000. Trade B, on the other hand, had a drawdown of $1,250 before recovering a little to lose $1,000. Both Trades A and B appear to generate the same profit, when in reality Trade A actually made $1,000 and Trade B actually lost $1,000. Whether the dollar amount indicated along the Y-axis is a profit or loss is deter-mined by the color and direction of the arrow.

> **Evaluation Tip**
>
> MAE can be calculated in either a dollar or percentage format. We have selected the dollar format for this example, but both formats were tested to ensure that a complete analysis was performed.

Keeping the trades clustered on the same graph makes it easier to figure out how much unrealized loss must be incurred by a trade before it typically does not recover. In other words, MAE tells us when to cut our loss because the risks associated with the trade are no longer justified. This MAE graphic gives us a great indication where to place our protective stop.

Notice that the majority of winning trades can be found on the left side of Exhibit 11 while the losing trades are spread out a lit-tle more with the majority found more on the right side of the graph. Notice as well that when a trade experiences a drawdown of at least $1,500 it typically continues to lose even more money,

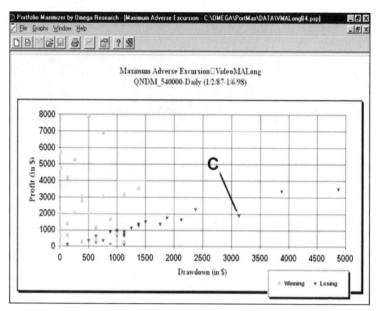

Exhibit 11: Maximum Adverse Excursion Stop Level

failing to recover. Take Trade C as an example. This trade had a drawdown of $3,100 but recovered somewhat to net a loss of $2,000. The beauty of MAE is that it shows that once a trade experiences a determined amount of drawdown we might as well stop out the trade. For our Deutsche Mark System that stop level is approximately $1,500.

Table 1 shows the performance results for the system when using a stop of $1,500.

Notice that applying the MAE stop not only improves our profitability by over 6% but we also lower our maximum drawdown by almost 5%. Although we have not discussed the RINA Index directly, notice that it increases dramatically by 36%. In summary, these results tell us that the system makes more money, takes on less risk, and is much more reliable with the application of the MAE protective stop.

Table 1: Maximum Adverse Excursion
Risk Management Strategy: MAE Protective Stop placed at $1,500

	Original	Adjusted	Difference
Net Profit	$33,250	$35,375	6.39%
Number of Trades	59	59	0.00%
% Profitable	47.37	45.76	(0.39%)
Ratio Avg. Win/Avg. Loss	2.25	2.57	14.22%
Profit Factor	2.03	2.17	6.89%
RINA Index	52.20	71.29	36.57%
Max DD%	18.75	15.69	(4.61%)
Average Trade	$583	$600	2.19%

MAE is a much more efficient way to determine a stop when compared to other subjective measures. This is because, in essence, we are letting the system's performance direct us to the most logical stop level. Now that we have applied a MAE stop to our system we can begin evaluating our system in more detail.

SYSTEM ANALYSIS SECTION

Our first evaluation section centers on the overall performance of the trading system and should be used to gauge the system's general performance. In other words, does the system make enough money to justify following its signals? We begin by reviewing a few key measures of system performance.

Net Profit

The Deutsche Mark system generated a healthy net profit of $35,375, a gross profit of $65,625, and gross loss of a little over

$30,000, all based on trading one Deutsche Mark contract over a ten year period.

Table 2: System Performance Measures

Net Profit	$35,375
Gross Profit	$65,625
Gross Loss	$30,250
Percent profitable	45.76%
Ratio Avg. Win/Avg. Loss	2.57
Profit Factor	2.17
Select Net Profit	$27,500
RINA Index	71.29

Percent Profitable

These are important numbers but they don't tell us anything about how we made the money. What we are really interested in is a few performance numbers.

This Deutsche Mark system was profitable in 45.76% of its trades. This number can be interpreted in many different ways. However, what we are looking for in a system is a percentage of 60% or more for non-trending systems and 35% or more for a trending systems as a starting point. In our case, because we are using moving averages to identify trends in the Deutsche Mark, we find a percent profitable of 45.76 acceptable.

Ratio Avg. Win/Avg. Loss

Another performance number is the ratio of average win to average loss. This number simply divides the average winning trade by the average losing trade to produce a ratio. Our system generated a ratio of 2.57. What you are looking for is a number above 1 as a starting point. Again our system is above our evaluation level.

Profit Factor

Our next number is called Profit factor. Profit factor is calculated by dividing gross profit by gross loss. It represents how much money was made for every dollar lost. Look for a system with a profit factor of 2.5 or more. Our system doesn't hit our performance goal but then again we haven't applied any money management to the system yet.

Select Net Profit

Select Net Profit is our next performance number. This figure adjusts the system's results by removing all positive and negative outlier trades. Systems that are heavily dependent upon outlier trades will have dramatically different net profit results than systems that do not. A trade is considered to be an outlier if its profit/loss is greater than three standard deviations away from the average. This calculation removes what we would consider to be good luck and bad luck trades from our analysis. Our Deutsche Mark system generates a very positive $27,500. This is less than the system's real net profit but its still quite good and very stable.

RINA Index

The RINA Index is our final risk measure that we will review. This index represents the reward-to-risk ratio per one unit of time. The RINA Index is calculated by taking the Selected Net

Evaluation Tip
The RINA Index will be used extensively to evaluate our system's performance once we apply a few money management strategies.

Profit divided by Average Drawdown which is then divided by the Percent Time in the Market. The larger the RINA Index the better the trading performance. Look for a system with an index of 30 or more. This is an extremely important performance measure that will be used extensively in the money management chapter. Our system produced a very healthy RINA Index of 71.29, well above our evaluation level of 30.

Before we conclude our general system overview, let's take a look at a detailed equity graph for our system. Equity graphs can tell us a great deal about the performance of our system over time.

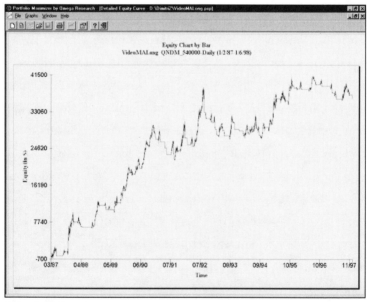

Exhibit 12: Detailed Equity Graph

This graph offers greater insight into trading performance because it displays net profit on a bar-by-bar basis revealing equity drawdowns and run-ups. Flat or non-trading periods are also shown to present a detailed overview of equity performance. Notice that our system has a strong equity graph that produces large consistent profit over time.

TOTAL TRADE ANALYSIS

Our next evaluation section centers on the system's individual trades. The total trade section takes the evaluation a step further by critiquing each trade made by the system.

Table 3: Total Trade Performance Measures

Number of Trades	59
Average Trade	$600
Coefficient of Variation	377%

Our Deutsche Mark trading system generated 59 Trades with an average profit of $600. Looking at our total trade numbers a little closer we see that our average trade of $600 is not extremely stable. The coefficient of variation for the average trade is 377%, which is quite high. Generally we like to see this number below 250%. But since we are dealing with a simple trend following a moving average system, this number is not that unusual. However,

Evaluation Tip
For more complete information concerning the interpretation of Coefficient of Variation refer to our Trading Stability tip in Appendix A.

if we had our way we would like to see this number lower. The lower the Coefficient of Variation the more stable the number. Coefficient of Variation expresses the standard deviation as a percentage of the mean. This percentage figure relates to the stability of the trades.

DRAWDOWN ANALYSIS

This section centers on the statistical evaluation of a system's drawdown. Drawdown is defined as the system's maximum loss potential during the course of a trade. The greater the drawdown, the more pain experienced by the trader.

Table 4: Drawdown Performance Measures

Maximum Drawdown	$1,625
Average Drawdown	$805
Coefficient of Variation	64%

Our Deutsche Mark system had an average drawdown of only $805 and its Coefficient of Variation was a very stable 64%. In this case we look for a Coefficient of Variation of 150% or less - which is accomplished in this case. More to the point, the maximum drawdown for an individual trade was only $1,625, which is extremely small given the history of the Deutsche Mark.

RUN-UP ANALYSIS

This section centers on the statistically evaluation of a system's run-up. Run-up is defined as the system's maximum profit potential during the course of a trade. Basically it's the opposite of drawdown. The greater the run-up the better the performance, assuming the system captures the majority of the move.

Table 5: Run-up Performance Measures

Maximum Run-up	$13,750
Average Run-up	$2,601
Coefficient of Variation	104%

The average run-up for the system was $2,600. Not that it captured all of that but it had the potential to make that dollar amount on average. The Coefficient of Variation for the run-up was 104% which is less than our 150% level for this number. Remember the lower the Coefficient of Variation the better. The System Maximum Run-up was a $13,750 high. But again we are dealing with a trend-following system so we should expect an occasional run-up of this level.

EFFICIENCY ANALYSIS

This section centers on a trade's efficiency to capture the maximum profit potential from the total price movement. The efficiencies are broken into three sections: entry, exit, and total. Trading systems tend to be relatively inefficient; even the best system does not take full advantage of each and every trading opportunity. This section is best used to improve system

> **Evaluation Tip**
> R For more complete information concerning Efficiency Analysis refer to RINA Systems' article, "Evaluating System Efficiency" published in the October 97 issue of *Technical Analysis of Stocks and Commodities*.

results either through indicator adjustments or money management techniques.

In its entirety the system does not trade very efficiently, but when we break our system down to the entry and exit efficiencies we quickly see a different story. Our entry signals are very efficient while our exit signals, less efficient. The strength to this system lies in its entry signals. This information will help us later in the money management stage.

The system's total efficiency was a negative 9.91%, which means that it made money but did so in an inefficient manner. Whenever possible we want the total efficiency figure to be in positive territory. Entry and exit numbers above 40% generally indicate a strong system. In our case the systems strengths can be seen in the entry efficiency number, which will help us improve our system.

Table 6: Efficiency Performance Measures

Total Efficiency	(9.91%)
Entry Efficiency	61.47%
Exit Efficiency	28.62%

TRADING SUMMARY

The trading summary section expands the general overview of the system's trading performance. In the previous sections the evaluation tools measured performance from the start to end during the test period. The next step is to examine the system over various time periods to ensure consistent performance. After all, what good is a winning system if a trader fails to follow it after its first loss? Remember consistency breeds confidence.

Evaluation Tip
For more complete information concerning Annual and Rolling Period Analysis refer to our Trading Summary tip in Appendix A.

The Trading Summary section is divided between Annual, Monthly, and Rolling period analysis. These various time periods are used to ensure the system's performance remains consistent over time. A mark-to-market is performed at the end of

each test period resulting in a complete and through performance evaluation.

Now before we get into too much detail let's address a question
that is frequently asked.   What does Mark-to-Market mean?
Let's explain.   Mark-to-Market is another term for closing the
books at a certain time. If a Mark-to-Market is performed on a
monthly basis, it means the account is officially closed at the end
of each month.   It is similar to receiving an account statement
from your broker with a bottom line on all open and closed positions.   This is important because without a Mark-to-Market it
would be impossible to know where profit or losses are to be
allocated.   Take for example a trade that makes 30% and that
begins November 1st and closes January 15th of the next year.
The Mark-to-Market allocates the proper percentages to each
month as opposed to the entire amount at the end of the period.
Without this simple accounting function it is impossible to have
a thorough and complete evaluation.

Trading Summary:			
Period	Net Profit	Profit Factor	% Profitable
98	($625.00)	0.00	0.00%
97-98	($3,625.00)	0.31	16.67%
96-98	($3,250.00)	0.53	18.18%
95-98	$6,000.00	1.73	38.89%
94-98	$6,625.00	1.59	42.31%
93-98	$4,750.00	1.27	39.39%
92-98	$5,000.00	1.20	35.90%
91-98	$8,500.00	1.29	35.56%
90-98	$15,375.00	1.47	37.25%
89-98	$23,750.00	1.71	39.29%
88-98	$24,125.00	1.83	38.71%
87-98	$35,375.00	1.93	40.00%

Source MONEY MANAGER by RINA Systems, Inc.

Table 7: Rolling Period Trading Summary

Now if we look at the rolling annual analysis of our Deutsche Mark system we see that the system results remain very consistent no matter when the system starts trading. Pay close attention to the Profit Factor and % Profitable figures and notice that they remain very stable over the rolling time period.

WINNING (LOSING) TRADE ANALYSIS

Our next evaluation section centers on the system's winning and losing trades. The same statistical measures used for total trades are used again on winning and losing trades to fine-tune the evaluation process.

Table 8: Winning and Losing Performance Measures

	Winning Trades	Losing Trades
Number of Trades	27	32
Average Trade	$2,430	$945
Coefficient of Variation	88.61%	57.09%

The number of winning and losing trades are about the same, but the average for winning trades is quite a bit larger than the average losing trade. The raw data that make up the ratio of average win to average loss can be seen here. But more important are the Coefficient of Variation for each number. Our system again generates very consistent numbers. We are looking of a Coefficient of Variation of less than 150%, which our system certainly meets.

EQUITY CURVE ANALYSIS

Our final section centers on our system's equity curve. Based on the detailed equity graph (Exhibit 12) our maximum equity drawdown figure calculates the greatest drawdown experienced by the system over time. It is then presented as a % or net profit at the time of the drawdown. This is a key performance measure used to evaluate risk.

Table 9: Equity Drawdown Performance Measure

Maximum Equity Drawdown (daily)	15.69%

Our simple Deutsche Mark system, although extremely stable, is not foolproof. Every system experiences some form of drawdown and our system is certainly no exception. This maximum equity drawdown measure is used to present the risks associated with trading a system. If a trader feels uncomfortable with the percentage drawdown then he should look for another system to trade.

Evaluation Tip
Maximum Equity Drawdown calculates the drawdown based on consecutive trades. This differs from the drawdown figure presented in the total trade section, which only looks at the largest drawdown for an individual trade

CHAPTER THREE SUMMARY

Our Deutsche Mark system has stable performance measures with a high Entry Efficiency and RINA Index and consistent run-up and drawdown figures. All in all we have a robust and profitable system that will become even more profitable once we begin to improve it with money management strategies.

chapter 4
Money, Risk & Equity Management

N ow that we have completed our system evaluation, we are now ready to improve the trading system through a variety of money, risk, and equity management strategies.

Money management is a process of altering trade size to achieve desired performance objectives. In its broader definition, it encompasses not only trade size, but also techniques that we call risk and equity management. Money Management can therefore be broken down into three different categories: Money, Risk, and Equity. These separate money management strategies are available in RINA Systems Money Manager software.

MONEY MANAGEMENT OVERVIEW

Money Management strategies are used to determine the position size to take on the next trade. These generally take the form of rules, which range from simple algorithms to strategies that optimize past performance to determine trade size.

A few Money Management strategies include:

- Martingale

- Anti-Martingale

- Losing Series

- Winning Series

- Fixed Fractional

- Optimal F

- Secure F

- Diluted Optimal F

- Fixed Contract Amount

RISK & EQUITY MANAGEMENT OVERVIEW

Evaluation Tip

RINA Systems created the video workshop entitled *"Portfolio Analysis and Money Management"* to cover applying money, risk, and equity management strategies in more detail.

While money management strategies help determine the number of contracts or shares to trade in the next position, risk and equity management strategies determine what to do while in an open position.

By applying risk and equity management strategies to a system, you may reduce the level of risk and thereby enhance the system's overall performance. This improvement may include an increase in profitability, a lowering of risk, or a combination of both.

Risk and equity management strategies include:

- Maximum Adverse Excursion

- Maximum Favorable Excursion

- Run-up Resistance

- Drawdown Support

- Underwater Equity Shutdown

- Equity Performance Scaling

As a trader, you don't want to take chances with your equity. If the market conditions aren't set up properly for your system, then you may want to liquidate positions and wait for another trading opportunity in order to minimize your losses. For the most part, Money, Risk, and Equity Management strategies enable you to increase the profitability of your trading system, while maintaining or lowering your risk exposure.

MONEY MANAGEMENT WARNING

Before we continue with our Deutsche Mark system we want to caution you on the proper way to use money management techniques. Like optimization, money management can be your best friend or worst enemy. If you attempt to impress people with astronomically large profits without regard to risk, you will defeat the purpose of money management. What we are about to explain is how to improve trading performance for practical real world trading. If we wanted to, we could easily impress you by turning our $35,000 system into a multi-million dollar system using ultra-aggressive money management strategies. However, that would merely be an exercise in pyramiding and curve fitting. Its great for show but just isn't practical to trade. So the bottom line is -- if it sounds too good to be true then it probably is. Any attempt to improve a system through the use of money management techniques must be followed by a complete and thorough system evaluation.

LONG DEUTSCHE MARK TRADING SYSTEM

Let's return to our Deutsche Mark system and begin improving it through the use of a number of money and risk management strategies. We will concentrate on the long side and later we will do the same for our short system.

DRAWDOWN SUPPORT

> **Evaluation Tip**
> The Drawdown Support strategy is most effective if the trading system is applied to have an Average Drawdown CoV figure less than 150% and Entry Efficiency greater than 40%.

Let's begin by improving our system with a realistic risk management strategy called Drawdown Support. You will recall that our long trading system was extremely consistent especially when it came to the various drawdown figures. More importantly, the system exhibited a high level of entry efficiency. This knowledge helps us determine strengths in our system that lend themselves to improving the overall system. These numbers basically tell us that the system occasionally enters into positions too soon, which causes it to experience some form of drawdown. Therefore, if the system experiences X amount of drawdown let's add to our open position. The amount of drawdown that must be experienced to allow us to add to positions can be answered with the use of a special graph and a little bit of testing.

The Drawdown Profit and Loss graph certainly helps point us in the right direction to improve our system.

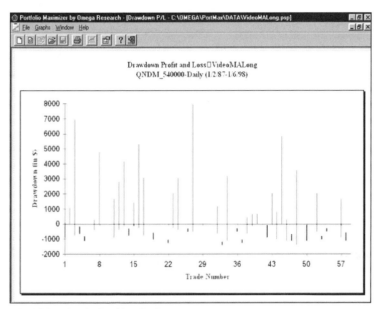

Exhibit 13: Drawdown Profit and Loss Graphic

What you are looking at in Exhibit 13 is a trade-by-trade bar chart showing each trade's maximum drawdown in comparison to its realized profit or loss. The low of each bar represents draw-down and the high of the bar represents the closed profit or loss. If the bar is light it made money and if it's dark it lost money. Look at trade 34 in particular. This trade was down as much as $1,125 at one time but was able to recover to net a profit of $3,125. If we were to add to this position when it was down $500 to $1,000, knowing that this system typically reverses from that drawdown level then we would make a heck of a lot more money with little added risk. Psychologically, however, traders seem to have difficulty adding to positions when they aren't making money. That's why in looking at this graph we can see an area of support for our trading system. When a trade loses between $500 to $1,000 dollars it has a tendency to recover. After a trade loses more than $1,000 it probably won't recover anyway and our Maximum Adverse Excursion stop discussed earlier will take over and liquidate the position.

This seems to be great but we don't trust anything unless we can crunch some numbers. So let's review the results of our trading system having added to positions once we are down $500 during the trade. To make this more interesting we have added not one contract but rather three contracts to take full advantage of our system's efficiency and drawdown characteristics.

Table 10: Drawdown Support
Add 3 contracts to the trade when a drawdown of $500 is experienced

	Original	Adjusted	Difference
Net Profit	$35,375	$138,875	292.58%
Number of Trades	59	105	77.96%
% Profitable	47.37%	45.71	(3.50%)
Ratio Avg. Win/Avg. Loss	2.25	3.02	34.22%
Profit Factor	2.17	2.74	26.26%
RINA Index	74.26	124.23	74.26%
Max DD%	15.69%	25.18%	60.48%
Select Net Profit	$27,750	$72,875	162.61%
Average Trade	$599	$1,322	120.70%

The Deutsche Mark system increases its net profit by almost 300%. At the same time our performance measures also improved; our ratio of average win to average loss increases by 34%, our profit factor jumps by 26% and most importantly our RINA index explodes by 74%. All of these numbers are impressive but we also have to think about risk. Our Deutsche Mark system is affected by an increase to our risk measure, namely Maximum Drawdown percentage, which increased by 60%. With all things equal, the positives far out way the negatives. What is most important here is that we must evaluate the pros and cons of this strategy and make our own decision.

WINNING SERIES

Let's turn our attention to improving the same system with a money management strategy. In this case the system has a tendency to make a fair sum of money in certain types of markets - mainly bullish markets. This is of course no surprise since this particular system only goes long the market. Logically then, once our system finds its trading niche we may want to increase our position size. Having said this, how do we know when our system has found its niche? Very simply, we evaluate the consecutive winning series for our Long trading system. The question that must be addressed is how many winning trades does the system need to experience before we increase our contract size?

By looking at the consecutive winning series exhibit we notice that the system had 4 different winning streaks. In each case the amount of

Evaluation Tip
The Winning Series Strategy is more effective if the trading system has large gains during a winning streak relative to the average loss that ends the streak. It also helps if the coefficient of variation figure for the average winning trade is less than 150%.

Consecutive Winning Series Data

Consec. Winners	# of Series	Average Gain/Series	Average Loss Next Trade
1	6	$3,208.33	($1,083.33)
2	3	$5,958.33	($958.33)
3	3	$6,583.33	($1,125.00)
4	1	$8,750.00	($750.00)

Source MONEY MANAGER by RINA Systems, Inc.

Table 11: Consecutive Winning Series

money made during the series was relatively large in comparison to the money lost on the trade that ended the series. We will need at least one winning trade to justify that the system is trading in a friendly environment. After that let's add one more contract after each winning trade up to a maximum of three contracts. Once a losing trade occurs we will return to trading one contract and wait for the next winning series.

Evaluation Tip
For more complete information concerning Winning Series Analysis refer to our Consecutive Trades tip in Appendix A.

The only reason we are adding to positions is simple -- the system has a tendency to do well during winning streaks. The system also has relatively small losses when the winning series ends. We are not saying that every system should apply this strategy, only those that have this type of trading characteristic. Besides we always test just to make sure our evaluation is correct.

Table 12: Winning Series

Add 1 contract after the first winning trade up to a maximum of 3 contracts and return to a single contract after a losing trade.

	Original	Adjusted	Difference
Net Profit	$35,375	$70,750	100.00%
Number of Trades	59	59	0.00%
% Profitable	45.76%	45.76%	0.00%
Ratio Avg. Win/Avg. Loss	2.25	2.84	26.22%
Profit Factor	2.17	2.39	10.14%
RINA Index	74.26	83.70	12.71%
Max DD%	15.69%	16.29%	3.82%
Select Net Profit	$27,750	$53,500	92.79%
Average Trade	$599	$1,199	100.16%

Take a look at the performance results once we apply our winning series strategy. These results show a 100% increase in profitability and only a small 4% increase in our Maximum Drawdown risk measure. Just as important our RINA index increases by almost 13%. All in all we make more money with little effect to risk.

FIXED FRACTION

The next step to improving our trading system is to combine money and risk management strategies together. In this example we will combine the Fixed Fractional money management strategy with our Drawdown Support risk management strategy introduced earlier.

Since the fixed fractional money management strategy is new -
let's first briefly describe it in some detail to fully appreciate its
true capabilities. The fixed fractional strategy invests a specified
percent or (fraction) of the capital in each trade, which is limited to the Margin requirement per contract. Now there are many
variations to the Fixed Fraction strategy so let's run through an
example to make sure we know how to calculate this version of
Fixed Fraction.

As an example, if your starting capital is $100,000 and the spec-
ified fraction is, say 20%, then only $20,000 will be invested
into the next trade. If the margin requirements are $10,000 per
contract and we have $20,000 to invest we can purchase two con-
tracts. Basically, the higher your equity grows, the more funds
you have available for trading and the more capital your system
can earn. The fixed fractional strategy enables a trader to man-

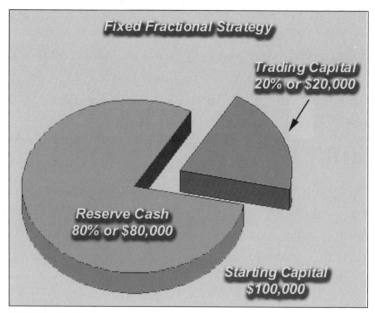

Table 13: Fixed Fractional

age positions by setting aside a portion of the equity. The advantage to this strategy is that it limits the amount of equity to risk, and allows the account to dramatically increase assuming the system traded is consistent and stable.

A consistent and stable system is exactly what we have in our Deutsche Mark moving average system. So let's apply our Fixed Fractional and Drawdown Support strategies to our system and evaluate the improvements.

First, we will use the same Drawdown Support inputs we used before but increase the number of contracts traded to a total of 5. Second, we will use a conservative 15% of our capital to

Evaluation Tip
The fixed fractional money management strategy is most effective with a consistent and stable trading system. Systems with volatile results should lower the fixed fractional percentage to reduce the impact of drawdown on performance.

Table 14: Money & Risk Management Strategy: FF & DS
Fixed Fractional 15% w/ $5,000 margin and Drawdown Support @ $500 adding 5 Contracts

	Original	Adjusted	Difference
Net Profit	$35,375	$256,500	625.08%
Number of Trades	59	105	77.96%
% Profitable	47.37%	47.62	0.53%
Ratio Avg. Win/Avg. Loss	2.25	2.18	(3.11%)
Profit Factor	2.17	1.98	(8.75%)
RINA Index	74.26	96.53	29.98%
Max DD%	15.69%	37.70%	140.28%
Select Net Profit	$27,750	$177,750	540.54%
Average Trade	$599	$2,442	307.67%

trade the Deutsche Mark based on a margin requirement of $5,000. With this said let's look at the results.

Notice that the system's net profit increases by 625%, but at the same time so too does one of our risk calculations. The Maximum Drawdown in percentage increases by 140%, but this is relatively small in comparison to the increase in net profit. More importantly, our RINA Index jumps by almost 30% a big improvement to the results of our long trading system. All of our other performance calculations basically remain unchanged including the % profitable ratio of average win to average loss as well as profit factor. A few of the other calculations actually increase in a positive manner. All in all, the system generates a lot more money with only a small increase to risk.

Well, if we like these results let's push the strategies to the limit to make as much money as possible. This after all is what money management is all about right. Wrong! If we push the system too much we will make the system overly aggressive and not worth trading.

To show you the effects money management can have on a trading system let's adjust our money management setting to make our system much more aggressive. We will use the same risk and money management strategies as we used before, but in this case, make the strategies trade more contracts.

The inputs for fixed fractional will be set at 50% of total capital and the margin requirement will be lowered to $3,000. These two changes will be the only alterations made to the money management strategies. These adjustments are basically telling the system to trade half of the available capital in every trade. That is extremely aggressive and most serious traders would agree that this is not terribly realistic. Now the only reason we are going to test these results is to prove a very important point. It's not how much money you make but how you make the money that is most important.

Table 15: Aggressive Fixed Fraction & Drawdown Support
Fixed Fraction set at 50% w/$3,000 and DD $500 adding 5 Contracts

	Original	Adjusted	Difference
Net Profit	$35,375	$2,246,625	6,250.88%
Number of Trades	59	105	77.96%
% Profitable	47.62%	47.62%	0.00%
Ratio Avg. Win/Avg. Loss	2.25	1.94	(13.77%)
Profit Factor	2.17	1.76	(18.89%)
RINA Index	74.26	17.90	(75.89%)
Max DD%	15.69%	49.41%	214.91%
Select Net Profit	$27,750	$35,9125	1,194.14%
Average Trade	$599	$21,396	3,471.95%

Take at look at these results in Table 15. The system now makes almost $2\frac{1}{4}$ million dollars; that's an improvement of 6,250%. Now we are talking some real numbers, but unfortunately this increase in profitability comes at a cost. Notice that the system's maximum Drawdown percentage increases well over 200% and more importantly the RINA index plummets by 76%. These numbers make it very difficult to get overly excited about these trading results. Making well over 2 million dollars sounds great but the risk reward ratios do not justify trading this system based on these aggressive money management settings. The reality is less is more when it comes to this particular trading system.

SHORT DEUTSCHE MARK TRADING SYSTEM

Up until now we have been concentrating on the long side of this Deutsche Mark trading system. Let's flip things around and refocus on the short side of our system. Now due to space limitations we won't be able to run our robustness analysis or detailed system evaluation on our short system, but we can skip ahead and improve it with a few money and risk management techniques.

MAXIMUM FAVORABLE EXCURSION

The first technique we will use on our short Deutsche Mark system is a risk management strategy called Maximum Favorable Excursion. Maximum Favorable Excursion or MFE is an analytical process that allows traders to distinguish between average trades and those that offer blockbuster profit potential. The advantage of MFE is its ability to recognize above average performance during a trade and therefore give traders an opportunity to enhance performance with the MFE risk management strategy.

Evaluation Tip
The Maximum Favorable Excursion strategy is most effective with systems that have a run-up CoV figure of 150% or less and an exit efficient figure of 40% or higher.

To assist in our analysis we will use a Maximum Favorable Excursion by Percentage graphic provided by Portfolio Maximizer.

The vertical axis represents the closed profit or loss for each individual trade. The horizontal axis represents the amount of unrealized profit

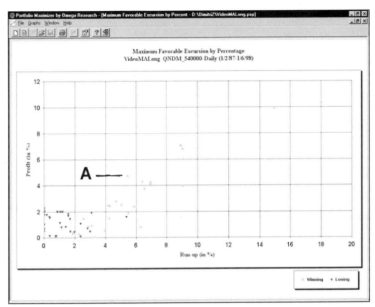

Exhibit 14: Maximum Favorable Excursion by Percentage

or run-up experienced by the trade during the life of the trade. To make the MFE analysis easier to interpret, both winning and losing trades are plotted on the same graph. The light up arrows represent the winning trades, while the dark down arrows represent losing trades. This graphic is similar to the Maximum Adverse Excursion presented earlier but rather than centering on drawdown this graphic centers on run-up.

The question we are attempting to answer is how much unrealized profit does a trade have to make before it typically generates a larger than average profit. Let's take a look at a specific trade to appreciate the MFE risk management strategy.

Trade A was up $5\frac{3}{4}$ % at one time during its trade but it fell back a bit to generate a realized profit of $4\frac{1}{2}$ %. Now because we can see that this system is stable all we have to do is add to positions once a trade makes more than X percent of run-up. Notice that the majority of losing trades falls between a 0 and 2% run-up. A couple of losing trades actually makes it up to 3% but this is certainly not the norm. So in evaluating this system, if we wait for a trade hit a 2% run-up before adding to the position, we should make a lot more money with little effect to risk.

This strategy works particularly well for trending systems, because when the system hits a bonafide trend we want as many positions on as possible.

Let's use Money Manager to test our MFE strategy to see if the risk reward calculations justify implementing this technique.

Table 16: Maximum Favorable Excursion
Add 2 contracts at the MFE 2% level

	Original	Adjusted	Difference
Net Profit	$43,000	$100,515	133.75%
Number of Trades	71	100	40.84%
% Profitable	45.07%	49.00%	8.72%
Ratio Avg. Win/Avg. Loss	2.03	2.30	13.30%
Profit Factor	2.21	2.70	22.17%
RINA Index	74.26	17.90	(75.89%)
Max DD%	12.91%	22.13%	71.41%
Select Net Profit	$26,250	$73,340	179.39%
Average Trade	$605	$1,005	66.11%

Our system's net profit improves by over 130%, the RINA Index rockets up over 85%, and our Maximum Drawdown % increases by 70%. All of our other calculations are improved making the system much more profitable relative to our risk measures. If a trader was unwilling to accept this increase in risk he could increase his trading capital prior to trading the system or trade fewer contracts or shares. Either way it's up to the trade to make the final decision whether to implement the strategy or not.

DRAWDOWN SUPPORT (SHORT SIDE)

Let's continue improving our short Deutsche Mark system with another risk management strategy. We will revisit our Drawdown Support strategy introduced earlier. We will use this same strategy to prove that it works for both the long and short system. In this case we will wait for a trade to lose $750 before adding 3 contracts to the position. Again just to reiterate, stock and mutual fund traders would add shares not contracts to properly apply this strategy.

Table 17: Drawdown Support
Add 3 contracts at the $750 Drawdown Support

	Original	Adjusted	Difference
Net Profit	$43,000	$127,750	197.09%
Number of Trades	71	115	61.97%
% Profitable	45.07%	45.22%	0.33%
Ratio Avg. Win/Avg. Loss	2.03	2.43	19.70%
Profit Factor	2.21	2.57	16.29%
RINA Index	79.22	200.95	153.66%
Max DD%	12.91%	17.41%	34.85%
Select Net Profit	$26,250	$85,750	226.66%
Average Trade	$605	$1,110	83.47%

The results of the drawdown support strategy certainly suggest that the system has been substantially improved. Our net profit increases by almost 200%, our RINA Index increases by over 150%, and our risk measure of Maximum Drawdown % only increases by 34%. This is a huge improvement to the simple moving average system.

OPTIMAL F

In addition to the strategies we have discussed thus far, there are several strategies that seek to find optimal amounts of a trader's capital to risk on each trade. The strategies we will discuss determine the optimal amounts of capital to invest, while doing so in a manner that keeps the amount of capital risked on each trade at a fixed proportion of total account equity.

In much the same way that trading systems can be optimized for entry and exit parameters, they can also be back tested to determine what would have been the optimal amount of capital to risk on each trade. Because traders have the opportunity to employ a variety of money management strategies it is useful to know what would have been the optimal amount of capital to invest in each trade. We will begin with a discussion of the strategy known as Optimal f and how it can be applied to trading. In addition, we will present a strategy developed at RINA Systems, known as Secure f, which attempts to overcome some of the limitations and problems associated with trading the Optimal f strategy.

Ralph Vince introduced Optimal f in his book *Portfolio Management Formulas*. The following excerpt clearly demonstrates the significance of determining the amount of capital invested in a series of trades.

As an example, let's imagine you have tossed a coin 3 times. You won the first two and lost the third. How much should you have invested if you had known that in advance? Obviously, the case is much simpler than the trading history but they have similarities. In the example above the correct answer without any other considerations is 1/3 of your money every time and you would have made slightly over 18%. If you had put 2/3 of the allocated money into every trade you would have actually lost over 7%.

This strategy determines, based on a sequence of past trades, the amount of equity to invest in each trade to yield the highest return. For a more detailed discussion of the mathematics behind the Optimal f strategy refer to Vince's book *Portfolio Management Formulas*.

The purpose of Optimal f is to maximize the final equity by investing the correct amount in each trade. This amount is f% of the existing equity at the time the trade is initiated. To find the value of Optimal f the calculations are applied to a set of historical trades. The history of trades must be profitable to derive any useful information from this strategy. Neither Optimal f, nor any other strategy, will turn a losing strategy into a winning one. The longer Optimal f is used the more final equity will result from its application, assuming that the additional series of trades have a positive expectation. However, this does not necessarily imply that a greater annualized return will be achieved by applying it over a longer timeframe. Also, we shall see that there are concerns of how Optimal f may perform on past trades and its persistence (that is, the value for f remaining stable) in future sequences of trades or outcomes.

Optimal f provides a geometric growth of capital for a trader that has a long series of successful trades. The geometric growth applies, however, not only to the profitability but also to the potential risk. The information gained from Optimal f is invaluable because it gives a trader the option to see the amount of capital required to invest in each trade to achieve maximum system results. In addition, you can learn whether optimal performance of a system is compatible with the amount of capital you intend to risk on each trade. Indeed, if possible, traders would benefit from trading at or levels slightly below the percent of equity to invest, as determined by the Optimal f strategy.

Several limitations exist, however, that have led to the limited use of the Optimal f money management strategy in the trading community. In fact, even for those who have tested the strategy, we seldom find traders who are actually willing to trade the percent of equity suggested by the Optimal f strategy. Perhaps the main limitation of the Optimal f strategy is that it requires the assumption that the nature of the data or input to the trading methodology will have the same characteristics in the future as it does in the base period. This means that a trader implementing Optimal f is making assumptions about the distribution and behavior of price in the past trades having some similarity to the nature and behavior of price in the future. Essentially this means that the nature of the data from which the buy and sell rules are derived (which of course determines our outcomes or profits) must be representative of what we can expect in the future. This may seem trivial because you can always assert that for any technical system to work it must make some assumptions of how the future will be related to the past. However, employing an Optimal f strategy may serve to magnify the effects by creating a geometric growth of capital that is built upon assumptions about the characteristics of the inputs (typically market price) in the past.   Also, if the value of the Optimal f shifts in the future, a substantial deterioration in results can occur quite quickly.   Exhibit 15 displays a curve demonstrating the relationship between net profit and the amount of capital invested in a trade for a set of theoretical trades. Notice the steep decline as the value of f moves to the right. An overestimation of the value for f when trading can prove to be catastrophic. Therefore, while it is a mathematical property that the Optimal f is the preferred amount of capital to risk on each trade for a systems trader using a fixed betting/ investing strategy, the implementation of this strategy can be quite difficult given the uncertainties between the properties of the inputs that generate outcomes (profits/losses) of trades during the period observed (base period) and future outcomes (real time trading). Or stated more simply, if the market changes and the system produces different profits (or losses God forbid) trading with the Optimal f from the base period may push the trader to the right on the Optimal f curve, possibly leading to disaster. Therefore, many traders have sought out ways to ensure that they remain to the left of Optimal f on this curve by employing many different methods ranging from a dilution of the value of f to adding constraints to the calculation of f. It is the latter method, that we have introduced (which we call Secure f) that we will discuss next.

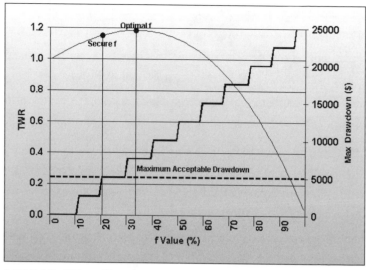

Evaluation Tip

The Optimal f/Secure f comparison graphic in Exhibit 15 was created using the Secure f Calculator which can be downloaded for free at www.rinasystems.com.

Let's apply the Optimal f strategy in combination with the Drawdown Support strategy and review the results of our Deutsche Mark trading system. In this example we will apply the Optimal f strategy based on $5,000 margin per contract and the Drawdown Support strategy based on adding 5 contracts once a trade generates a $500 unrealized loss.

The results in Table 18 show a dramatic improvement but at a cost to our risk measure. The Net Profit figure increases by over 1,700% but our Maximum Drawdown percentage calculation increases by almost 300%. This increase in risk will most likely prevent the typical trader from following this aggressive strategy despite the impressive $800,000 net profit return.

Table 18: Optimal f & Drawdown Support
Optimal f set with a 10 trade base period and a 5k margin and Drawdown Support set at a $500 level adding 5 contracts

	Original	Adjusted	Difference
Net Profit	$43,000	$803,375	1,768.31%
Number of Trades	71	126	77.46%
% Profitable	45.07%	53.97%	19.74%
Ratio Avg. Win/Avg. Loss	2.03	1.49	(26.60%)
Profit Factor	2.21	1.75	(20.81%)
RINA Index	79.22	96.52	24.99%
Max DD%	12.91%	49.37%	282.42%
Select Net Profit	$26,250	$488,625	1,761.43%
Average Trade	$605	$6,375.99	953.88%

SECURE F

Secure f is a money management strategy that uses a fixed bet size to determine how much capital to invest in a trade. It is similar to Optimal f in every respect except that it introduces a drawdown constraint. Because of a trader's inability to accept the drawdown often associated with trading at optimal amounts of capital and because of the risk of overstating the value of f in the base period, we designed a method that gives a trader the ability to subject Optimal f to constraints.

An essential difference between the two strategies is that Secure f incorporates price analysis into its calculation. This is accomplished by

> **Evaluation Tip**
> For more complete information concerning Secure F refer to RINA Systems' article, "Secure Fractional Money Management " published in the July 98 issue of *Technical Analysis of Stocks and Commodities.*

including the constraint on drawdown in the Secure f calculation. Therefore, it goes beyond factoring in only the entry and exit points of a trade. What happens during a trade (more specifically, the drawdown incurred) is included into the calculation of Secure f. We find that many traders are concerned not only with where the trade was entered and exited, but also with the fluctuations in price during a trade.

As with Optimal f, Secure f allows the trader to see the optimal amount of capital to invest in each trade to achieve the highest return, subject to the drawdown constraint. Secure f, however, gives the trader the ability to calculate an optimal fraction of the capital to invest with an acceptable amount of drawdown. Therefore, instead of simply viewing whether the value for f is consistent with the trader's risk tolerance, the trader can make the value for f compliant with his comfort with risk.

If the value of the maximum trade drawdown is set higher or equal to the maximum trade drawdown during the trades, then the result will be the same as in the case of Optimal f. If the value for f is set too small it will limit the capital and profitability of the strategy causing too many trades to be prematurely exited/stopped out. A primary benefit of this strategy is that it can be made to be as aggressive or conservative as the trader wishes, depending on the drawdown constraint selected.

Evaluation Tip
The Secure f strategy is best applied to systems that produce consistent results with an Average Trade CoV less than 250% and an Average Drawdown CoV less than 150%.

Let's apply the Secure f strategy to our system using the exact same setting used for the Optimal f strategy and review the results. As you can see in Table 19 the Secure f generates a smaller net profit figure than the Optimal f results in Table 18 but the results still reflect better all around performance. The system's Net Profit increased by over 1,100%, the RINA Index increased by almost 120% and percent profitable increased by almost 20%. The downside to this improvement is the increase to our risk measure Maximum Drawdown percent, which increased by 140%. With all things considered the systems performance is definitely improved. The improvement, however, must be weighed against a trader's risk tolerance.

Table 19: Secure f & Drawdown Support
Secure f set with a 10k drawdown limit and a 10 trade base period with 5k margin and Drawdown Support set at level $500 adding 5 contracts

	Original	Adjusted	Difference
Net Profit	$43,000	$503,250	1,133.14%
Number of Trades	71	126	77.46%
% Profitable	45.07%	53.97%	19.74%
Ratio Avg. Win/Avg. Loss	2.03	1.95	(3.94%)
Profit Factor	2.21	2.28	3.17%
RINA Index	79.22	173.48	118.98%
Max DD%	12.91%	30.90	139.53%
Select Net Profit	$26,250	$357,000	1,260%
Average Trade	$605	$4,208.33	595.59%

FIXED FRACTION (SHORT SIDE)

Let's continue with the improvement stage and apply a few money and risk management strategies to our short Deutsche Mark trading system.

Similar to the improvement techniques applied to our long system, let's do the same to our short system. In this example we will use Fixed Fractional and Drawdown Support strategies to improve our trading system.

In this case we are allocating 30% of our capital to trade the Deutsche Mark based on a margin requirement of $7,000. We will also add 3 contracts to our position when it experiences a drawdown support level of $750.

Table 20: Money & Risk Management Strategy Fixed Fractional & Drawdown Support
Fixed Fractional set at 30% with 7k margin and Drawdown Support set at level $750 adding 3 contracts

	Original	Adjusted	Difference
Net Profit	$43,000	$319,590	643.23%
Number of Trades	71	136	91.54%
% Profitable	45.07%	49.26%	9.29%
Ratio Avg. Win/Avg. Loss	2.03	1.65	(18.71%)
Profit Factor	2.21	2.03	(8.14%)
RINA Index	79.22	144.97	82.99%
Max DD%	12.91%	42.23%	227.11%
Average DD	$848	$2,800	229.82%
Select Net Profit	$26,250	$214,590	717.48%
Average Trade	$605	$2,349	288.26%

Combining these two strategies makes a significant improvement to our trading system. Our net profit figure increases well over 640%, and the % profitable figure increases by 9% to stand at almost 50%. Fifty percent winners for a simple crossover system is pretty good. Our RINA index also improves by over 80%. Our risk measure maximum drawdown % increases by 227%, but given the fact that net profit increased by 643% the risk measure increase is acceptable.

Now if we wanted to be ultra-aggressive we can improve the system but, as always, we have to take into account our risk measures. If we were to change our fixed fractional setting we could easily improve our net profit figure by 5,400% but this would come at a cost to our RINA index and max drawdown % measures.

Table 21: Aggressive Fixed Fraction & Drawdown Support
Fixed 50% with 3k margin DD $500 Add 5 contracts

	Original	Adjusted	Difference
Net Profit	$43,000	$2,468,125	5,439.82%
Number of Trades	71	126	77.46%
% Profitable	45.07%	53.97%	19.74%
Ratio Avg. Win/Avg. Loss	2.03	1.56	(23.15%)
Profit Factor	2.21	1.83	(17.19%)
RINA Index	79.22	39.74	(49.83%)
Max DD%	12.91%	58.69%	354.61%
Average DD	$848	$37,694	4,345.04%
Select Net Profit	$26,250	$581,125	2,113.80%
Average Trade	$605	$19,588	3,137.68%

Take a look at these results and you will see that although net profit appears to improve in reality, the risk measure tells a different story.

Combining these strategies together generates a huge improvement to the system's net profit but our RINA Index falls by almost 50%. As soon as we see a decline in the RINA index of this magnitude, it's probably a safe bet that our performance results are going to suffer. Take a close look at these numbers and you will see that the system is now extremely aggressive and not worth trading.

CHAPTER FOUR SUMMARY

Each of the money management examples we have used has improved our performance results. These improvements do not stem from a simple increase in profitability but more importantly from conclusive analysis of a variety of risk/reward calculations. It is not enough to say I've made more money therefore I've improved my system. A realistic improvement must include the trading characteristics of the system and the risk tolerance of the trader. Improving a system without regard to risk may be acceptable to a few ultra-aggressive traders, but the rest of the trading community must apply money management techniques in an appropriate manner to ensure that we feel comfortable with our trading system.

Now that we have improved our separate long and short Deutsche Mark moving average systems, the next stage is to combine them together. To accomplish this task we will create and analyze a small moving average crossover Deutsche Mark portfolio using Portfolio Maximizer. The portfolio in this case will contain two components, a long trading system and a short trading system.

chapter 5
Portfolio Analysis

The final step in the creation of our trading system is to join our two systems together into a portfolio. Now even though we could have developed a single system inside of TradeStation, we have deliberately separated our two systems. Why? Because we wanted to evaluate and improve the systems separately to build the most profitable portfolio possible.

Creating our overall system or portfolio in this format offers us two distinct advantages.

First, evaluating and ultimately improving the systems separately allows us to develop a stronger methodology that effectively trades both bullish and bearish moves independently to capitalize on human nature driven by greed and fear. What works in a bull phase may not work in a bear phase and vice versa.

Therefore developing two separate systems that join together to create a portfolio allows us more control at both the evaluation stage as well as the improvement or money management stage.

Second, creating our portfolio in this format allows the independent systems to trade at the same time. Systems that trade both long and short in TradeStation cannot trade simultaneously. A system that is long cannot go short until it has completed its long signal. Therefore the system could miss a perfectly sound short signal solely because the system was still in a long position.

Separating the systems allows the portfolio to trade more efficiently.

LONG AND SHORT DEUTSCHE MARK PORTFOLIO

Let's take a look at the separate systems and see how they combine to create our Deutsche Mark portfolio.

Both systems evolved from the same trading methodology to generate very similar trading results. The system's net is $78,000 based on trading only two Deutsche Mark contracts, one for the long system and one for the short. The systems combine to produce a % profitable figure of nearly 50% - pretty good for a moving average system. More importantly, the ratio of average win to average loss, profit factor and RINA Index all show signs that we have a profitable portfolio. The bottom line is we have a very strong portfolio that is now capable of trading the DM in both bullish and bearish markets.

Table 22: Portfolio Long/Short Original

	Long	Short	Portfolio
Net Profit	$35,375	$43,000	$78,375
Number of Trades	59	71	130
% Profitable	47.37%	52.11%	49.23%
Ratio Avg. Win/Avg. Loss	2.57	2.03	2.26
Profit Factor	2.17	2.21	2.19
RINA Index	74.26	79.22	73.81
Max DD%	15.69%	12.91%	14.30%
Select Net Profit	$27,750	$26,250	$54,640
Average Trade	$599	$605	$602

PORTFOLIO WITH APPLIED MONEY MANAGEMENT

The next step is to join our individual systems together after having applied our money and risk management strategies.

Table 23: Portfolio Long/Short Systems with Money Management

	Original	Adjusted	Difference
Net Profit	$78,375	$576,090	635.04%
Number of Trades	130	214	64.61%
% Profitable	49.23%	51.87%	5.36%
Ratio Avg. Win/Avg. Loss	2.26	1.86	(17.69%)
Profit Factor	2.19	2.01	(8.22%)
RINA Index	73.81	116.99	58.50%
Max DD%	16.76%	25.12%	51.02%
Select Net Profit	$54,640	$392,340	618.05%
Average Trade	$602	$2,390	297.01%

CHAPTER FIVE SUMMARY

As you can see our portfolio dramatically improves with our net profit soaring 635%. Our % Profitable improves to over 50%. Our RINA Index also improves by almost 60%, a dramatic increase. On the downside our ratio of average win to average loss and profit factor both decease and our Max % DD increases. However, we find this acceptable given the improvements made to our performance figures. Now that the two systems have been combined together we can see the positive effects of our money and risk management strategies.

Conclusion
Stage Review

Now that we have constructed a portfolio and examined the results, we have completed all of the necessary stages for designing a winning trading system.

Before we finish let's briefly review what we covered in this workshop case study.

First, we designed a trading methodology, seeking to exploit some tendency of the underlying market. In our case, we looked at the DM, which falls into the trending category.

Next, we developed a simple system using moving averages to take advantage of the Deutsche Mark. We also separated the system into long and short to better trade this market.

Having established a system, we began the process of evaluating our system using robustness analysis to determine stable system inputs. After finding a stable setting for our system we evaluated the performance with Portfolio Maximizer to find the strengths and weaknesses of the system.

Having determined that we have a sound trading system in place we focused on improving the trading system using both money and risk management. We were able to achieve substantial improvements by using strategies such as Drawdown support, Fixed Fractional, and Maximum Favorable Excursion, just to name a few.

Finally, we combined our long and short Deutsche Mark systems into a portfolio to analyze how they interacted.

Whether you decide to follow these stages verbatim or adapt them to your needs we think you will find this process helpful in improving your trading. Using the stages we covered today you can:

- Determine the stability of your system.

- Objectively evaluate the performance of your system.

- Improve your system's results with innovative money and risk management tools.

- Combine systems into a portfolio that meets your objectives and trading profile.

We feel confident that the information in this book will help you maximize your ability to improve trading systems that match your trading style and objectives.

Good luck in your trading. If you have questions concerning any of the material covered in *Profit Strategies: Unlocking Trading Performance With Money Management* please feel free to contact RINA Systems at: Tel. (513) 469-7462 or Fax (513) 469-2223.

Appendix A

TRADING STABILITY

Let's begin our evaluation of total trades by comparing the results of two systems. On the surface both systems listed below appear to be the same, with identical figures for net profit, total number of trades, and average profit per trade. Beneath the surface, however, lies a different story.

	System A	System B
Net Profit	$100,000	$100,000
Total Trades	50	50
Average Trade	$2,000	$2,000
Standard Deviation	$714	$5,335
Coefficient of Variation	35.71%	266.78%

Notice the differences between the standard deviation and coefficient of variation calculations for the two systems. These numbers measure the volatility of the average trade. The greater the volatility the less stable the average. Both systems had the same average $2,000 profit per trade. The trades associated with System A fluctuate around the average in a tight range. Based on its standard deviation of ±$714, the average trade should range between $2,714 and $1,286. System B on the other hand has a standard deviation of $5,335, which translates into trades that range between $7,335 and ($3,335). These are dramatically different numbers for systems that appear to be the same. The net result is System A is the more stable system.

The systems can also be evaluated based on their coefficient of variations. This statistical measure is similar to standard deviation - the smaller the figure the more stable the trades. Coefficient of variation is calculated in a percentage format allowing for easy interpretation between systems. Look for systems with coefficient of variations of 250% or less. Numbers larger than this should be viewed with a certain amount of skepticism.

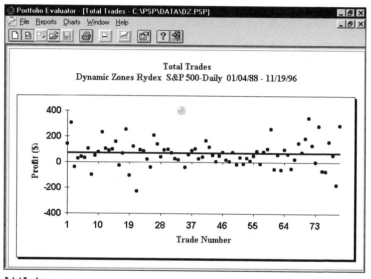

Total Trades

It's easy to get lost in these numbers. Sometimes it's best to review these statistical results in a graphic format. The chart above plots the individual trades for the Dynamic Zones Rydex System. Notice the clustering of data points. Very few trades deviate from the average. The one exception was trade number thirty-four. This type of trade is considered to be an outlier and will be discussed in greater detail in the next section. Despite this one outlier trade, the standard deviation and coefficient of variation for this trading system was $108.26 and 154.11% respectfully. These low values reflect a system that is extremely stable in relation to its average. This high degree of stability breeds trading confidence.

CONSECUTIVE TRADES

Short-term trading confidence, or lack thereof, quite often stems from the number of consecutive winning and losing trades produced by a system. After a winning streak, you can become overly confident and believe that your system is infallible. After a few losing trades you can become easily discouraged, risk averse, and perhaps, are even reluctant to trade. In any case, the trading principles behind your system have remained constant, while your perception of the system has changed. By tracking the performance of consecutive trades, you can gain additional insight into the personality of your system and thereby trade with greater confidence.

Let's begin our discussion of consecutive trade analysis with a definition. A series is defined as a sequence of winning or losing trades that occur in consecutive order. The streak ends when a trade results in a gain or loss in the opposite direction of the series. Calculations based on consecutive series data can produce two very powerful evaluation tools:

1. Average gain or loss for the series.

2. Average gain or loss for the trade that ends the series.

These tools help you analyze your system's performance, during and after a variety of trading situations. They also serve as a historic reference for future trades. The first calculation takes an average of all the trades that occur within the consecutive series. This figure can determine a system's profitability during periods of extended strength or weakness. The longer the series, theoretically, the larger the average gain or loss.

The second calculation centers on the average return for the trade that ends the series. This figure can determine how abruptly a system reverses its course of action after a consecutive series. A small losing reversal is preferred for a winning series, while a large winning reversal is preferred for a losing series. The object after all is to end the consecutive series with the smallest loss or largest gain that is possible.

Let's take a look at the consecutive winning series for our sample CCI Spike trading system. A description of this system, including the TradeStation code, can be found on our web site. All numbers are quoted in S&P 500 Index points.

Consecutive Winning Series

Consec. Winners	# of Series	Avg. Gain/Series	Avg. Loss Next Trade
1	4	9.40	(4.15)
2	3	8.48	(2.44)
3	1	25.64	(2.21)
4	2	30.05	(1.65)
5	2	31.67	(1.12)
6	0	0.00	0.00
7	0	0.00	0.00
8	1	31.99	(0.42)

This system generated a number of consecutive winning trades, and as expected, the longer the series, the larger the average gain per series. Notice the inverse relationship between the average series gain and the series ending trade. As the average series gain increased, the series ending trade actually decreased. In this case, when the system wasn't trading in sync (i.e. few consecutive winning trades), the loss on the series ending trade was relatively high. However, when the system was able to accumulate a few consecutive winning trades, the loss that followed was relatively low.

The trading rationale is simple--a system that trades exceptionally well (i.e. numerous consecutive winning trades) has most likely found its preferred trading zone. In other words, the system is running on all cylinders. It would be unusual for a system that is trading "red hot" to immediately turn "ice cold." The more likely scenario would have the system end its winning streak based on a relatively small loss. This is the mark of a well-designed system. Knowing a system's historic tendency during and after a consecutive series of trades will help you build confidence in your trading system.

As a speaker at a Bridge/Telerate TAG Conference, I heard a number of market related stories. One story in particular fits nicely with our discussion of "real world" Consecutive Series Data analysis.

An investor, after months of comparing trading services, finally decided to subscribe to a trading service with an impressive track record. The service was in the midst of a small winning streak, making the investment decision all the easier. As time passed the service continued to extend its winning streak. The investor, thrilled with the results, felt reassured in his decision to subscribe to the service. After a few more winning trades, the investor began to feel a little uneasy, knowing that all winning streaks must eventually end. As the winning streak persisted, the investor completely centered his attention on the next losing position. The more the service won the more uncomfortable the investor became. Eventually the investor, consumed with fear of a major loss, decided to pull out of the service. When asked why the investor had left the service the response was why wait for a major loss?

It is important to remember that the only thing that changed in this case was the investor's perception. Who says that the next losing trade had to be a major loss. If the system had been evaluated using the consecutive series data in the first place, then the investor would have been better prepared to trade the system. Fear of the unknown always weighs heavier in our mind than that which is known. Preparing for the unknown begins with a thorough system evaluation.

TRADING SUMMARY

The most common approach to evaluating a trading system consists of a general overview. This form of evaluation reviews the performance of a system only at the end of the test period. The next step is to dissect a system over various time periods to ensure consistent performance.

A concerted effort to fully evaluate your system may flush out hidden strengths or weaknesses not readily apparent. Three simple evaluation methods provide a unique insight into your system's true performance. The greater the detail, the better the perspective you will have on the system. A word of warning -- never rely on any one time frame in your review.

Portfolio Maximizer provides instant access to the following evaluation methods:

1. Annual -- Searches for pockets of strength or weakness.

2. Rolling Period -- Searches for extended periods of strength or weakness.

3. Equity Curve -- Provides a graphic of the system's performance over time.

Let's take a look at two trading systems to better understand the advantages of dissecting a system over various time frames.

Yearly	Total	'98	'97	'96	'95
System A	80K	20K	20K	20K	20K
System B	80K	10K	90K	(15K)	(5K)
Rolling	Total	'98	'98-'97	'98-'96	'98-'95
System A	80K	20K	40K	60K	80K
System B	80K	10K	100K	85K	80K

Both systems generated the same net profit over the same time period; however, the paths taken were distinctly different. System A was extremely consistent, while System B was more volatile. Without this extended review, both systems would appear on the surface to be the same. This added detail serves to critique the system in an effort to better match the personality of the trader to that of the system. The results provide greater insight than that of the general overview.

However, note that this analysis does not attempt to rank the performance of these systems, but rather simply point out potential differences between the systems. In addition to net profit, a number of other evaluation tools (i.e. % gain, profit factor, and % profitable) are also used by Performance Summary Plus in the trading summary analysis.

Viewing a system's equity curve can also provide some additional insight into its performance. Equity curve charts tally a system's individual trades and present a time line of trade-by-trade results. The chart examines the same basic yearly and rolling period information, but does so in a graphical format. A quick review of an equity curve chart can provide the needed mental security to trade any system. Until you see your system's equity curve, you never know what's really at stake.

About the Author

David Stendahl is Vice-President of RINA Systems, Inc. a leader in portfolio analysis and money management software. David has contributed to the development of RINA Systems' portfolio evaluation, money management, and trading software, which includes Portfolio Maximizer, Money Manager, 3D SmartView, and the Dynamic Zone indicator.

A frequent speaker at national and international conferences, David presents workshops that concentrate on improving trading performance. He has also authored numerous articles on evaluation and money management techniques. David has also co-authored *Computerized Trading: Maximizing Day Trading and Overnight Profits* (ISBN 0-7352-0077-7), edited by Mark Jurik and published by the New York Institute of Finance. An active trader David specializes in trading S&P futures, OEX options and specialty mutual funds following a mechanized trading system.

Trading
Resource
Guide

∞

Tools for
Successful
Money
Management

Suggested Reading List

The New Money Management: A Framework for Asset Allocation, by Ralph Vince - Introducing a remarkable asset allocation system that brings an easy-to-follow rigor to previous models of investment selection and timing. Learn to accurately measure the benefits & consequences of a trade before committing to it - which dramatically increases your odds for success.

224 pp $65.00 Item #2835

New Market Wizards, by Jack Schwager - Meet a new generation of market killers. These hot traders make millions - often in hours - and consistently outperform peers. They use vastly different methods, but share big successes. Now, you can meet them and learn their methods. How do they do it? How can you do it? Learn their winning ways with this bestseller.

493 pp $39.95 Item #2106

Technical Analysis of the Financial Markets, by John Murphy - From how to read charts to understanding indicators and the crucial role of technical analysis in investing, you won't find a more thorough or up-to-date source. Revised and expanded for today's changing financial world, it applies to equities as well as the futures markets.

542 pp $70.00 Item #10239

Maximum Adverse Excursion: Analyzing Price Fluctuations for Trading

Management, by John Sweeney - Maximum Adverse Excursion (MAE) helps avoid potential losses before making a costly trading decision, replacing guesswork with statistical calculations that enable you to quantify the loss point in advance. MAE's creator shows how to: Make charts to measure market behavior, determine capital requirements for every trade, manage investment risk daily - everything you need to profit from this amazing tool.

168 pp $49.95 Item #2555

New Trading Dimensions: How to Profit from Chaos in Stocks, Bonds and

Commodities, by Bill Williams - Introduces a new method of market forecasting that combines traditional technical charting methodology with chaos theory and psychology. Includes in-depth and understandable explanation, direction and analysis of oscillators, fractals, AC signals and more. Practice problems, case-studies and tips to get you started.

260 pp $59.95 Item #10105

McMillan on Options, by Larry McMillan - Brand new "Bible" of

the options market from the world's leading expert gives a complete game plan for trading options. Learn McMillan's best strategies and hedging techniques, with full instructions on how and when to use them. Going way beyond the basics, it's being called "the best options book currently available."

570 pp $69.95 Item #2678

Trading the Plan: Build Wealth, Manage Money, Control Risk, by Robert Deel

- How much should you risk in any one trade? How much leverage should you use? Answers to these and other tough questions on investing, managing money and limiting profit-draining losses.

220 pp $49.95 Item #6979

Design, Testing & Optimization of Trading Systems, by Robert

Pardo - Hands on guide to building, refining and trading your own computerized trading system. Regardless of which technical software you use, you'll learn to choose the right indicators to suit your risk tolerance and profit goals. Discover how to combine a wide range of indicators and analysis methods to compliment each other. Pardo, a pioneer in trading system development, walks you through the process of refining, testing and trading your chosen system.

176 pp $49.95 Item #2171

Important Internet Sites

Traders' Library Bookstore - www.traderslibrary.com, the #1 source for trading investment books, videos and related products.

RINA Systems - www.rinasystems.com, the leader in the development of performance analysis software for traders and investors.

Bridge Financial - www.crbinex.com, a comprehensive source of products and services for futures and options traders. This "one-stop" site offers current quotes, on-line data, books, software products, news and information - from one of the world's leading financial information source.

MurphyMorris - www.murphymorris.com, The site of Technical Analysis gurus John Murphy and Greg. Morris. A perfect site for both beginners and those more experienced in Technical Analysis.

Wall Street Directory - www.wsdinc.com, the best director of financial sites on the web. A comprehensive source that will help you find the answers to all your financial questions.

Dorsey Wright - www.dorseywright.com, The source for information on Point & Figure analysis and comprehensive Point & Figure charts.

Equity Analytics - www.e-analytics.com, An excellent educational resource with extensive glossaries for technical analysis and many other topics.

FutureSource - www.futuresource.com, a comprehensive source of information for futures and other traders providing futures quotes, settlement prices, charts, FWN news, chat rooms and other useful tools for traders of all levels.

Futures Magazine - www.futuresmag.com, filled with information for futures and options traders, plus books, videos and dates of their popular trading conferences.

Track Data - www.tdc.com, a supplier of electronically delivered financial data since 1981 - with several services specifically designed to assist day traders. Timely market data, financial data bases, historical information, data manipulation tools and analytical services are available.

Conferences & Seminars

RINA Systems Workshops

RINA Systems' workshops are designed with one goal in mind -- to give you the tools and knowledge necessary to analyze and improve trading performance using rigorous evaluation, money management and asset allocation techniques. RINA Systems gives you the competitive edge.

Workshop Topics

There are many key components to a successful trading plan. Two of the most important parts are your trading system and your money management strategy. David Stendahl will show you how to evaluate a trading system so you can find a system that matches your individual trading style. From there he will discuss several money management strategies designed to improve trading performance. You'll be amazed as David demonstrates step-by-step exactly how to apply a variety of money management strategies on fully disclosed trading methodologies.

- The Big Picture
- Performance Evaluation
- System Design
- Money Management

For more information on these conferences call RINA Systems at 513-469-7462 or visit us on the web at www.rinasystems.com and download our free demonstration software.

Telerate TAG conference

For over 20 years, TAG (Technical Analysis Group) has presented annually 3-days of balanced workshops for new and experienced traders alike. Structured to give you a firm foundation and keep you abreast of the latest research and techniques, TAG helps you further your technical analysis education in a structured environment designed to teach. Learn to trade with confidence and get hands-on instruction from the industry's top traders.

For information contact: Tim Slater, 504-592-4550

Futures West & South

Twice yearly, Futures Magazine Group presents 3-day conferences featuring in-depth presentations by trading experts, plus an exhibit hall showcasing the newest products and services for traders. You'll find everything related to trading in an intimate, hands-on setting that allows you to mingle with the experts. With tracks for beginning, intermediate and advanced trading - something is offered for every active trader.

For information contact: Russ Koehler, conference director   800-221-4352 or 312/977-0999

Omega World

The growing trend toward system trading is clear and OmegaWorld is the premier conference dedicated to system trading and development. Those willing to take more control of their investment program will find of wealth of information, along with workshops geared towards beginning and advanced attendees. Serious, in-depth sessions, exhibits of the industry's top products and latest software and lots of exciting events make this a stand-out event for all traders.

For information contact: 800-327-3794